Sunflower Equations

Sunflower
Equations

June English

Hearing Eye

Published by Hearing Eye 2008

Hearing Eye
Box 1, 99 Torriano Avenue
London NW5 2RX, UK
email: books@hearingeye.org
www.hearingeye.org

Poems © June English, 2008

ISBN: 978-1-905082-34-6

Acknowledgements
Some of these poems have appeared in the following magazines;
Acumen, Agenda, Equinox, Envoi, The Interpreter's House, Orbis, Poetry Nottingham,
Quattrocento, Trespass, in the newspapers Independent on Sunday and Morning Star,
and anthologies Images of Women and Statement for the Prosecution.

Printed and bound by Cambridge University Press
Hearing Eye is represented by Inpress Ltd in the UK – see www.inpressbooks.co.uk
and trade distribution: Central Books, London E9 5LN
Designed by Martin Parker at www.silbercow.co.uk
Sunflower drawing by Emily Johns and cover design by Martin Parker

Contents

Experience

Between Worlds

I'm flying face-downwards through
a cylindrical tunnel; electrical storms
explode, lightning-flashes glance off metal
surfaces, startled fireballs roll, erupt,
the metallic clang of closing doors
bombards my eardrums;
gale-force winds blast my cheeks,
whip my hair to rats' tails,
flatten my hands against my thighs
as I torpedo westwards –
portholes thunder shut, leaving me
with snapshots, flashcard impressions
of past lives, vacant worlds,
a nineteen forties living-room,
an empty nursery, a cluttered kitchen,
computer stations – scanners, printers – onwards,
gathering speed past a deserted playground,
a country church, a wooded hillside
thick with snow, towards
                    a chrysanthemum of yellow light.

Twenty, nineteen, eighteen, seventeen,
she's coming back – sixteen, fifteen,
she's almost there, fourteen, thirteen –
my heart drums against my rib-cage –
twelve, eleven – the helicopter whirr
of a bee's wings and its body bouncing
off the window, mad bent on escape – *ten, nine,*
come on, you can do it..... I open my eyes,
note tubes, drips, the doctors bending over me;
a nurse is rubbing my hands, another
supports me as I turn my face to greet
the sun's warmth, crying
                    for the living hell of it.

Different

Mum hangs me upside down and taps
my lungs to make me cough and spit,
she always says *I'm sorry love.*
Is that what other mothers say
after they've played the tip-tap game?

Mrs Rutter, Yvonne's mother
says Mummy coddles me too much,
a bit o' muck 'd do me good.
She'd have no can't do this or that,
if I was 'ers I'd smarten up!

I don't know why I'm always ill,
Yvonne Rutter never is —
I bet her Mum's a better thumper.
Maybe I should smarten up,
it's hard to run, but I could try.

***

It's summer now, Yvonne and I
are playing 'camps' in Blackman's quarry,
Snotty Robert's got a cold. Mum
said, *You'd best stay clear of him,*
but he's the Daddy in our game.

Yvonne, who's Mum, is belting me,
and shouting, *Smarten up, or else*
but Snotty Robert slaps her one
and says, *it's bed-time, git to bed*
so I lay down, pretend to sleep.

***

I don't remember getting home,
it seems the milkman carried me.
Mum said, *You silly girl, the ground
was damp, you've taken chill.* My head's
a blazing furnace, filled with dreams:

*I'm walking barefoot over mountains,
a devil's prodding me with knives,
I'm lost. Alone. I'm terrified —
the mountain's gone, it's forests now
I'm running fast, my lungs will burst.*

Mum leans the folded ironing board
lengthways from settee to floor;
she holds my toes while I slide down
to play my *Walk-on-ceilings-game*,
where lights grow upwards from their stalks

and little folk, with chalk-white faces
(only seen by Mum and me)
play silly games, like *Wonder why.*
I asked them once why pigs don't fly —
they said because they've learned to swim ...

***

Mrs Rutter's been to see me,
she says I'll soon be up and running,
if I was hers I'd smarten up,
a bit o' muck 'd do me good —
I'd like to poke my tongue at her,

but Mum is smiling down at me,
that knowing look that tells me *Don't —
the folk round here don't understand,
you're different see — a special girl.
When you grow up, you'll show them all...*

As You Sow

1

Dig-Dig grew flowers, 'cherryanthus',
love-in-the-mist, 'jam-tarts', asters;
we'd sell them as we walked back home,
through that fifties prefab jungle –
shilling a bunch, ninepence to mates
he stopped to joss with, free to some:

It does no 'arm t'gi' a few
away: Ma Bingly 'an't got two
'apeth to rub together – Martha
Ricks lost her Fred a month or so
ago, I doubt she'll see another
soul t' cackle wi' till Monday.

2

Dig-Dig was hush-hush stuff at home
for things I wasn't old enough
t'know. Outlawed, he camped in our
front parlour. Grandma kept her bed-
room locked – he kipped in his armchair –
I used to wonder if they kissed.

Years later, Mother whispered things
that made no sense or seemed untrue,
that left me hung between the two –
she'd been abused, she told Grandma;
Dig-Dig lied and she'd been punished –
how to believe, or disbelieve?

3

Dig-Dig was kind to all my friends,
he never moaned and shouted hush.
Marie and Josie thought him fun,
we played at Hide and Seek and Tag —
Mum's half-hatched warnings left me cold —
he was my pal, my champion.

Then suddenly, no friends came round,
I wasn't welcome at their house.
Mum's questions were beyond my ken —
she said Dig-Dig had done bad things,
I felt the ground beneath me crack:
how to believe, or disbelieve?

4

The family did their level best
to freeze him out when folk popped in,
but he felt morally obliged
to do his bit; he'd bare his chest
and scratch it with a bristle-brush,
screech, *Look at me, I'm bloody fit.*

Two nuns called one afternoon.
Stripped to the waist, he flexed his muscles.
Mother Annunciata twinkled,
Sure, it's a fine figure of a man ...
Mother Keiran bit the bullet,
Crossed herself and said, *Amen.*

Soon scolded out, we both retired,
to dance a polka down the hallway,
plan an outing to the pictures —

The Plaza's showing Key Stone Cops —
si' thee borrow a thrupenny bit,
we'll tek jam slammers for us tea.

5

Did he touch you in the shouldn'ts —
the lowered voice, the needling probe —
I'll swing for him, I swear I will;
while I, too young to understand
the ins and outs, squirmed my silence,
preferring Dig-Dig's bouncy fun ...

Sixty years and I'm still puzzled,
(how to believe, or disbelieve?)
The old-child man I loved so much,
my step-grandad, my pal, the friend
who danced with me and played at tag,
or mum, who loved me over life?

Kitchen Front

Grey cobbled streets and ragamuffin kids,
Snotty Robert and Yvonne Rutter's gang
circle like hungry hounds around their prey —
a bedraggled girl clutching a banana.

Inside, a paltry fire spits and burns,
three lumps of sooty coal, our wartime ration
while Mam dries tea-leaves for a second brew
and Grandpa tunes the wireless for the news:

six carrots, 1 oz. of margarine, oatmeal,
1 gill of milk, 1 oz. of cornflour,
fat for frying, seasoning to taste.
Leave till cold then shape into croquettes.

Outside, the mob have moved in for the kill,
the victim's knickers wave a grey surrender,
as Snotty Robert pins her by her pigtails,
and Yvonne Rutter grabs the chomped banana.

Time Slot

This is the alley where time slots still,
where wives and mothers weep and wave
as soldiers, sailors kiss goodbye
and children sing their skipping songs:

Touch your collar, never swallow,
never catch a fever...

This is the alley that calls me back
to ration books, make-do-and-mend,
gas-masks slung on weary shoulders
and fresh bread rising in the hearth.

This is the alley where memories live,
where Jack the coalman humps his load,
and Adam Jenkins plays spitfires
while Jennifer Hardy skips:

Touch your collar, never swallow,
never catch a fever...

This is the alley that Hitler missed,
though he got the church two lanes away
and the butcher's that sold rabbit pie
with hopes of a sausage or two.

This is the alley where baby Rosie
lay fighting a feverish sweat,
twisting and writhing and turning
on the coldest of winter nights.

Touch your collar, never swallow,
never catch a fever...

This is the alley where Rosie died –
alone in the cobblestone house,
pinned to her cot with safety pins,
while Mummy jived with G.I. Joe...

Bloody War!

Bloody War! Oh what a palaver -
clickety-clack of knitting needles,
khaki socks and balaclavas,
ration-books and blackout curtains.

> *Spitfires chasing Messerschmitts,*
> *shells that rip the town to bits.*

Learning to read in one-roomed schools,
carrying gas-masks, endless queues,
sweetie rations and tasteless gruel,
borrowed boots and cut-down clothes.

> *Sirens shrieking, helter-skelter,*
> *bedding down in the air-raid shelter.*

Chocolate-brown and cream emulsion,
tea-leaves saved for second brewing,
scrambled eggs from cardboard cartons,
tablecloths of day-old news.

> *Glenn Miller's jazz and Little Brown Jug.*
> *Damn and blast, it's a Doodle-bug.*

Crackle and hiss of frugal coal fires,
Saturday Playhouse on the wireless,
Valentine Dyall *The Man in Black*,
ghoulies, ghosties and bumpety-bumps.

> *Sirens shrieking, helter-skelter,*
> *bedding down in the air-raid shelter.*

Scrubbing collars, boiling sheets,
fresh bread rising on the copper;
spit and polish and elbow-grease,
black-lead, beeswax and well-buffed brass.

Spitfires chasing Messerschmitts,
shells that rip the town to bits.

Praying that we'll see tomorrow.
And another round of beg-and-borrow.

Recurring Dreams

...of Crowther Street, the sitting room,
table, rent-book, three half-crowns,
a makeshift bed with clean white sheets.

I'm four years old and itchy-hot,
Keep her in bed, the Doctor says:
I slither out and steal the rent.

The lino's red and smooth and cold,
smooth and cold as the bony hands
that soap my face and scour my skin.

The bony hands are Grandma's hands:
she drags me down on the old red floor,
and severs my hand, my small white hand –

blood flows out from the severed hand,
that lifted the lino and hid the rent...

I'll Be Your Sweetheart

Remember me? Valentine Dyall,
your *Man in Black*.

Yes. I thought so. Once seen...
It was a dark and stormy night
in the winter of 1942...

Grandfather Roberts was there, hush
and you'll hear the creak of his rocking-chair,
the clink of his glass. He'd taken
his boots off, stood them beside
his bottle of stout. Listen to the coals spit.

Your eyes were scared open,
your body corkscrewed around
a feather pillow. You were six
then, a golden haired child,
with the curves of a Raphael angel;
one cherubic hand clutched a rag doll,
the other pressed against your mouth
as if to stop the scream.

I was telling a story about a child
who invited a man into the house.
I'd got to the part where the carrion crow
screeched from the rafters when
the sulphuric acid accumulator failed –
the wireless died.

Grandpa Roberts was furious
but I didn't mind. I didn't mind
because you could feel my breath
on your neck as you walked up the shadowy staircase
to your low-ceilinged room...

Silent Spy

I'm following my cousin and some chap:
they're checking, making sure no one's in sight.
My job's to figure out exactly why —
we're on the cliff path heading for the sea —
they're the target, I'm the *Silent Spy* —
I saw it at the cinema last night.

9.20 — suspects whispering together,
they've crept off down a side-path, looking sly
(they're what Gran calls well matched, 'birds of a feather').
This spying's perilous, but 'do or die'.

Look out, they've gone to ground and so have I —
I wonder if they're pestered by these ants?
I catch their voices, but the words aren't clear —
Her pet lip's shown itself — he's looking sulky
murmuring secret things that I can't hear.
What's bulging in the pockets of his pants?

9.26 — He's flushed and so is she,
this could be it, although I'm not sure what!
I'm creeping nearer now, agog to see —
if that's a gun in there I might get shot!

I wonder what the heck he's up to now?
It could be double fireworks tonight!
Hang on! He's after something in her bra —
and now he's got her in a stranglehold,
should I step in before things go too far?
She's putting up a very feeble fight.

9.30 — time to tell them trouble brewing —
I've got them cornered now, I'll make them pay.
I'll get the ins and outs of what they're doing,
or charge them half a crown to go away.

Double Reverse

We've taken most of her right lung.
The left is scarred. She'll always have
a cough. Just twenty-one — that young —
I doubt she'll ever dance again.

Twenty yards of lilac tulle,
skirt gathered to a hand-span waist,
the bodice seamed with whalebone spills,
lined throughout in rustling satin —
and not a hope in hell she'll wear it.

Take it steady, walk a hundred
yards or so. She doubled it,
stopped. Pushed half a mile, ignored
the telling pain, the warning cough.

And so the family rallied — choked
through their fears to spur her on:
determined she would have her moment.
Mum, Dad, sister, Gran and Grandad,
glueing sequins, auguring dreams.

Stand on the stool so we can see.
Can you believe how well she looks?
Claps and cheers and Grandad singing,
'*Just the way you look tonight*'.

Heart quickening in its whalebone cage,
sidestep, chassé, swish of skirts,
double reverse and oversway —
                    poised on quicksilver ...

Riversflow

(A haven on the River Dour)

The undertaker wants Dad's shoes. The thought
of him just lying there, his pin-stripe suit –
and best white shirt, his work-worn naked feet –
probably shouting, *Where's my bloody boots!*

He always called shoes *boots.* I polish them
and stow them in my bag. *It's time to go;*
how strange it seems, knowing I won't see him,
won't hear his *Giddy up to Riversflow...*

My hands shake as I close the door. *Don't cry,*
I tell myself, *You've got a task to do.*
Dad's face appears, pastiched on passers-by;
I know he's dead, but can't believe it's true.

The streets seem changed, until I pass the Co-op.
Stop. Go back, gather courage, look inside,
believing, in that moment, that he'll pop
his head out, call, *I'll see you later, mind*

you tell thee Mum I've bought scrag-end of lamb.
But he's not there. I hug his shoes and stride
with more determined steps. It won't take long –
five hundred yards, turn left, bear right, then straight...

I'm ushered in, spoken to in low, slow tones,
asked, *Would you like to see your father now?*
His waxen face and hollow cheeks, stark bones,
owe nothing to the Dad I love and know –

he's all of that and more at Riversflow:
the sun's his warm embrace, the rustling leaves
his *Well done, thank you, love.* The kiss he blows
a fragrant *See, I told thee not to grieve...*

April 10th, 1965

Thirty-seven years ago today:
an indrawn breath of disbelief —
that juddering sense of
dislocation...

Yes. I recall the exact date,
the precise time I found your ring
(with a cheque to cover household bills),
set down beside my photograph

and how my mind formed fortress-gates
that kept me marching round and round,
answering those worn-out questions,
like how? and why? and later on, with who?

And still the tenderness that was
reminds me of the days we lay beneath
the strong Sidari sun and how our breathing
merged when our two bodies cleaved as one
with the sonorous sounds of surf.

Cameo

I was your first experiment in colour,
you'd only snapped in monochrome before,
how fortunate I'd chosen to wear floral.
My dress? A challenge of overstated pinks.

A scenic courtship, nothing flashy,
your sapper khaki, and my fifties prints,
the sun, the moon and Margate sands,
the swift embrace – the wayward tide –

a guard of honour in army blues
for my white-satined dreams,
the man and wife on our wedding cake
recorded in your Brownie Box.

The snaps kept under cellophane:
a black and white of me in pinks
and you in battledress and boots.

Winged Fruits

1

Thirty-three years ago,
that long-haul flight to Canada,
our fresh-start hearts carved on the arbutus.

The seeming steadfastness of sun,
those unadopted roads we didn't take,
beaches begging for our footprints,
grasslands, giant redwoods, forests of pine:
your late night business dinners,
lipstick on your shirttail.

Those burnt-out flames of fall,
and silent months of snow.

So when apple blossom perfumed May
and the Oregon wore fervent white,
there was no warmth, no rebirth bloom,
for we were out of song, off key.

It takes a shyster to sham summer,
you did it beautifully. I revelled
in the panoramic blues and greens
of thawed lakes and sudden streams
until we hit the Klondike trail
and headed North towards Alaska –
late night parties with your drinking *buddies*,
the *other women* you explained too well …

2

In England now;
the lonely journey through the Rockies,
the boat that shipped me slowly from your side
almost forgotten — *my tongue*
sinks deep into Sugar Maple,
tastes the honeyed moment of its leaves,
absorbs the sweetness of the sap, homes in
on a syrup too golden for a jar...

A Marriage

1

Whiffen Spit, Vancouver Island, 1966

I see you now,
black curly hair, leopard eyes,
on the harbour side of the lonely spit,
chain-smoking Players Weights,
with an eye on your watch...

I see you now,
in your red-check shirt,
your lumberjack boots,
kicking dried cuttlefish, scuttling crabs,
near a swarm of wasps on a squashed apricot.

I see you now,
fag in hand, skimming stones,
when our youngest was stung,
when he screamed with pain,
when he wet his pants.

I see you now,
standing cool and unmoved –
while I cleaned him up,
and we cleared away –
like a bit-part actor in a boring play.

Family Day, June 1967

A picnic on the beach
at Whiffen Spit, you and me,
a chance to build those bridges,
the ones that Father Fahey
talked about, but didn't show us how.

Our sons paddling in rock pools,
excited by seaweed and snails;
me calling, *See what we've found.*
That moment, when the world spun
and you stood still.

The picnic, laid out in Tupperware:
brown-bread sandwiches, prawn and tuna,
little one shouting, *Come and get it.*
The offered plate still hanging there...

The three of us, huddled together,
our eldest bringing the bag,
helping me through in his grownup way.
Wanting you with us, fearing the words
 you didn't speak...

You on the harbour side, unapproachable
as the bald eagle warily stripping flesh
from a beached Chinook salmon.
                    Ready to fly...

3

Thanksgiving, October 1970

You at Whiffen Spit, on the seaward side,
where the Cascade Mountains rise
in sheeted skies, like the demented
ghosts of wedding cakes, where hawks
and turkey vultures flay the air.

Too quiet, our children's play
in this graveyard of the sea. Pensive,
they sift the bleached bones of cuttlefish
and conch, find a calcified starfish,
ask me why it doesn't swim.

You move to the harbour side, examine
sheltered rock pools where small fish
dart and hide in seaweed gardens,
find a sea anemone, a pulsating cell, red
as a woman's vulva, and poke it with a stick.

Later, in the shell called home,
you strip me, tie me, camera poised,
kneel between my quivering knees,
thrust screwdrivers into my womb,
skewer the woman from the girl.

Whore Games

Talk about sex, scandal and locked doors,
fishnet tights and bare buttocks,
rumpy-pumpy on the ironing board
with you in your Argyle socks.

Talk about me playing the fish-wife,
screeching for a taste of your cod;
talk about settling for whelks,
when I find that the cod's served cold.

Talk about playing at whore games
with you as an ironmonger,
and me on a bed of nails,
pretending I'm good at yoga.

Talk about power struggle,
talk about wolves baring fangs,
talk about vixens as playthings,
talk about hammer and tongs.

Talk about sex, scandal and locked doors
with you as a power-monger,
talk about bullies and bond-slaves
and the death of anger.

Talk about me as your whore,
mocked, degraded and beaten.
Talk about talk: you couldn't,
and my blouses cover the blows.

Nursery Rhyme

Our marriage was a Fairy Tale:
I stayed at home, you chased the Grail

or maybe it was Puss in Boots
whose tarts you filled with home-made fruits.

Miss Muffet woke this morning, sick
from playing Pat-a-Cake with your prick.

You're Jack-the-Lad, that rotten sod
who tumbled Jill and thinks he's God.

You popped the weasel, I suppose,
and that's the way the money goes.

I'm sick of playing with Tom Thumb
while others pull Jack's biggest plum.

I'm sick of hearing Boy Blue's horn
calling the meadow cow to corn,

and being cast as wicked Queen
while you eat fat and I eat lean.

At last Jack's learnt! He's not that quick −
he burnt his balls on the candlestick.

Negatives

I ought to burn these photographs,
flame my anger till it ashes,
return the memories un-kissed
to particles of household dust.

But when I close my eyes you're there,
as if something inside me wakes
and switches on a 3D screen.

Sunlight warms my darkened box
as searing white opposes black;
yellow, orange, violet, red
soar to life as you walk back,
a click, a whirr, before freefall,
then virtual reality is all —

what use is burning photographs
when you roam free on my brainscape
and I'm boxed in, with shutters closed,
the negative that you exposed.

The Violin Maker

(For my uncle James Dooley)

Year after year he sat cross-legged,
penknife in raw-boned sailor's hands
(roughened by years of cable-laying)
whittling away at the wood, slowly
shaving and shaping a block of pine.

> She got the gist: forty one pieces
> glued together, book-matched pine
> for back and sycamore to curve
> the breast, Canadian maple bridge –
> ready-made pegs and catgut strings.

He camped out in the basement, studied
Stradivarius, *His Life and Works*.
Using resin from the tung tree,
and mineral mixes high in silica,
he made – and exploded – varnishes.

> She lived with the smell of lacquer,
> 'in white' violins resting on sideboards,
> wood shavings and sea shanties –
> the catacoustics of strained strings
> that scratched her home-grown melodies.

Sometimes, when his children called,
he'd swing the baby shoulder-high
and dance a jig, till one by one
they all joined in and she would smile,
aware his work would call him back –

It's time to birth a Dooley violin,
a masterpiece of hand and eye;
he's tuning notes, exploring scales,
she's found the resin for his bow.
His eyes are closed, his spirit soars

in bird song — *The Lark Ascending...*

Stepmother

I hate the word, the scene it sets:
the wicked queen, the poisoned apple
and all the ugly things that people say,
You'll rue the day you took her on,
she'll run you ragged, drive you nuts...

For Christ's sake can't you see –
her mother's dead. She's broken down
with grief and fear; and I'm scared too –
not sure I've got the guts and skill
to love this nightmare through.

Her mother's dead. She's lost. Alone.
It's all her fault, she's *sure* of that,
and here I am, her father's wife,
a stranger in her mother's bed,
with new ideas and different ways –

sirens screech, it's World War Three,
it's all too much and far too soon;
she quite likes me, but fears the worst –
her Grandma says my smile's a front –
and I'm no saint, she's clipped my halo:

her socks aren't white, her hair's a mess,
she hasn't got a thing to wear,
her father's bought me this and that,
she doesn't like the food I cook,
she wants it plain, no fancy stuff.

I ask her if her Mum cooked pasta,
she pulls a face and says, *No thanks.*
I say, *Let's sit and make a menu,*
Monday's your choice, Tuesday's mine,
beg her show how her Mum did things;

and for a while I think I've cracked it,
till Christmas when all hell breaks loose:
she thinks my decorations cheap,
too much tinfoil, too much glitter.
She's rung a bell, I freeze her out —

then from the corner of an eye
I watch her sew a square of cloth
using chain-stitch as I've shown her,
and with a new-found tenderness
I reach towards her, hug my daughter.

Lullaby

(For my Granddaughter Cerys)

Cuddled close to Huggy-Hippo
crocheted into Johnson's slumber –
Cerys in her Moses basket,
dreaming of the grand awakening.

Mummy, kneeling, kisses baby,
crocheted into Johnson's slumber.
Nanny, Grandad, waiting, watching
mindful of the grand awakening –

sleepless nights and rattle-throwing –
Mummy, kneeling, kisses baby,
crawling, toddling, such a poppet.
Nanny, Grandad, waiting, watching

wobbly steps and *Whoops-a-daisy*,
sleepless nights and temper tantrums!
Painting, drawing, numbers – counting –
tricking Grandad, *such a poppet*:

little Miss Sophistication,
poised and ready – *Whoops-a-daisy*,
Grandad holds her by her cardie.
Painting, drawing, numbers – counting –

dressing up in Nanny's sparklers,
little Miss Sophistication –
caught on camera, time suspended.
Grandad holds her by her cardie,

little woman in the making,
dressing up in Nanny's sparklers –
caught on camera – time suspended,
cusped between naïve and knowing...

Grey

There is a certain heft of grey
in late September skies
that gathers into warning pockets
as shadows do on lungs —
but here today, in Normandy,
colours have more to say.

A soft pink glints the quarry face
— remaindered by the sun —
where, from jagged slits in granite crags,
rough shrubs and gorse bloom on
beside late pennywort and thistle
to vie for pride of place.

Wind-blown, a dandelion spreads
its broad-based leaves, umbrella-
shaped on grit, while hollow stalks
exhale their spheres of seed —
soon parachutes will clock and float
a host of yellow-heads.

Now gulls and wrens and magpies wrench
warm fruits off tangled briars
and from their muck new shoots will flower
in cracks on walls and cliffs;
while I am contemplating grey
brigades of blooms entrench.

Orphic

... it's the hoped-for jolt of it, you see —
speedwell, granny's toenails, cowslips
whole fields of them waiting for your feet.

You're starved of colour, see?
The darkness folding you in,
coal-dust in your eyes, your nose, your ears
you and a pick hacking at a black seam

You're half a mile down,
half a mile from life —
but sometimes...

I've brought it for thee,
carved it from t' pit face,
a fossil —
that were alive once.
Been lying there, dying there, millions of years,
locked in darkness.

Goa

Group Greeting

Welcome to Majorda Beach Resort,
five-star deluxe hotel — to the lushness
of its landscaped gardens, the azure blue
of warm Arabian seas, the endless
miles of soft white beach. Imagine,
Vishnu's magic arrow raising Goa,
from an under-bed of silvered sand.

Explore the grounds, rest in cool groves,
or under bright umbrellas, succumb
to sounds of surf and plucked guitars —
walk long sandy beaches fringed in palms,
enjoy the quirky Goan humour,
bamboo shacks like *Marks & Sparks*, buy
a beach wrap or a hand-carved elephant.

***

We chose the *Goan Hilton* — dined
bare-footed on the cooling sand —
grilled seafood and a fresh shore breeze —
watched the waves draw back, rise, hollow
and snake-like zigzag phosphorous shine.

Then, bowing to the cradle-quarter moon,
we scurried to our lavish room, leaving our
scraps to the hovering pack of feral dogs ...

Day Trip

We took a taxi, drove to Mazda Market,
arrived slow-style behind an elephant,
drowned in sun-bright hibiscus flowering
beside impoverished shacks and smart bazaars,
where sad-eyed women sat cross-legged
alongside stalls set out with silken saris –
turquoise, yellow, cyclamen, cerise –
and craftsmen offering plain and jangling bracelets,
effigies of Krishna, Shiva, Buddha.

Boat Trip

Squash on board a landing craft, prepare
to cross the Mandovi River, keep your cool
as muddied water swamps the Plimsoll line
and deck-hands joke, *we've lost a few like this...*

The dark-eyed baby's fingers found my hair,
I glanced upwards, admired the gold neck-rings
that elongated his mother's neck and smiled,
We women know and understand
as she untangled his small hands.

Guided Tour of Panaji

Welcome to Panaji, English name Panjim,
observe the influence of the Portuguese,
the Baroque splendour of the city's major church,
Our Lady of the Immaculate Conception,
with its ornate balustrades and towers.
Note the Latin lines of red brick houses
the well-laid gardens, the many statues
and avenues lined with acacias and gul mohar.

Our afternoon schedule includes a tour
of the ancient Adilshahi Palace;
later, after tea, there will be a chance to shop
along 18th June Road, do mind the potholes
in the pavements! Don't get lost, stay together —

I wander off, go left, not right —
        and find myself besieged by throngs
        of sari'd girls toting waxen, doll-like bundles;
        my shout awakes their babes — scrawny, bird-like
        mouths open on a cry I can't forget.

———————

OTHER VOICES

Sabbath

(For Alison)

I've come to terms with living death,
learned to play the M.S. game,
the two steps forward, ten steps back.
What I need now's a benison –
if you can truly walk on water,
feed five thousand with two fishes,
lend my hands the strength to paint –

the odds aren't great. I've little hope,
but if you *did* raise Lazarus,
heal the Centurion's man by proxy –
for all my sakes, let the Botox work –
let science have its miracles,
do it so my blindness sees.

I'm sick to death of vassalage,
my palette waits, I need your help
to recreate myself through colour,
in gold and red and aubergine,
ripe blackberries and stubble-fields.

I'll travel where my brushstrokes take me –
portray the Magdalene in crimson silk,
meet John the Baptist, arms outstretched
to rebirth me in Jordan's waters –

I'll portray the Red Sea's buoyant flow –
draw the leper you made whole,
paint a path towards my Maker.

We'll sit at God's right hand and share
the marriage wine you changed from water –

and on the Sabbath day I'll rest.

Crossings

Fugue

All night he lay in feverish sweat.
Fighting back her tears, she held his hand
until the reddened dawn relit
the shrouded ward, haloing
      his white sick bed.

The sunlight bothered him, frail fingers
fiddled with the sheets; she whispered
loving words. He twisted, gasped,
battled for breath; the rasping sound
      filled her with dread.

Gentle nurses checked his pulse,
his forehead creased, his cheeks caved in,
pale eyes found hers, his pupils quickened –
as if welcoming the break of day.
      Stilly red –

his eyelids set. On his locker,
carnations – a blaze of true scarlet –
the red picked up the rawness of his lids.
Glazed eyes flickered, focused, gathered them,
      his eyelids bled.

She touched him with her fingertips
      and knew him dead ...

***

Sonata

I picture you wrestling with the Russian Vine,
the easy way your shoulders rose and fell,
and how your hands worked rhythmically in tune
as if you heard an unplayed melody –

the way you'd turn and look at me and say,
Remember when I walked you home from school?
and how I'd watch you carefully shape the hedge –
the easy way your shoulders rose and fell.

And how on summer nights we'd sneak away,
out-walk the hedgerows till the rising hills
unfurled a bed of fragrant camomile;
and how your hands worked rhythmically in tune –

to rouse latent sonata chords in me;
and how your tempo matched itself to mine
as movements followed movements, slow but sure .
until you read crescendo from my score ...

Washed Up

The forecast offers prolonged frost
with temperatures below zero,
but she still hung out their washing,
stood and watched it blow.

Wondered, as it slowly froze –
sheets flattened, pillow slips – free-
dom fighters belled by wind? His socks,
iced up for kicking, cuffed her knee-

length leggings – such odd contrasts:
cartooned for duty, his working jeans
manfully bonked her *sensible* skirt,
bared its creased, frayed lining. Hasbeens,

that skirt and top – frozen reminders
of those flat-fish post-natal blues.
Wan smiles, headaches, and please be quick,
shapeless pinnies and flattie shoes;

those jeans show off his best assets.
Meaty, she thought, blowing warm air
through frozen palms. Maybe it's time
to think of spring, to streak my hair,

buy sexy see-through thongs and skirts
with slits to thigh and tops that tease,
rewrite our love in vibrant shades,
and launch it on an April breeze.

Eye Shadow

I'm a woman who's lost something,
something most important to her.
She had it on her wedding day,
but she couldn't tell you what.

She's a woman who has searched for it
on soap-powder and nappy days,
in feeding bottles and teething rings,
and sometimes got a peek at it.

She's a woman who has looked for it,
at netball games and football matches,
in school bags and school holidays,
but never really cracked it.

She's a woman who still searches for it,
and sometimes feels the thrill of it,
in novels from the library
which vaguely seem to hint at it:
but she couldn't tell you what.

Boxing Match

Why stick people in boxes,
label them *Mad, Interesting, Slime Ball,*
etcetera, etcetera? As if the rest
of them don't exist. For Gawd's sake
pull yourself together, you're turning
into a carbon copy of Dad, always
analyzing, making notes, filing them away.

Like that guy you call Pu, the one
that's mixed up with nuclear power.
Plutonium TOP SECRET stuff.
I gourmandize over his biceps,
write sonnets to his nethers
and all you can say is Pu's okay,
terrific scientist, great teacher,
convincing advocate for Nuclear Standoff...

What's up with you girl? Can't you see
he's droolable, fit as in sexy,
well nice as in wow.

Take a bit of sisterly advice,
look in the mirror. You've still got
all your bits and pieces in the right place,
so, unless you've got management
stamped on your buttocks, I'd say
it was time to jump out of the filing cabinet:
Pu plus you equals 'BIG BANG'.

Pu is the symbol for Plutonium (Pu: atomic number 94)

Dancing Ragtime to the Blues

I wasn't born to hug a bucket
or foxtrot with a vacuum-cleaner.
I don't cha-cha with feather-dusters
or tango with the carpet-beater.

I'm not cut out for playing wifey,
cucumber sandwiches etcetera.
I'd rather be a belly-dancer
and wear a ruby in my navel
than tango with a carpet-beater.

I've had my share of scraping ovens
with hands that feel like saucepan-scrubbers.
I'd rather woo a bullfighter
and ball fight through the pasodoble,
than cha-cha with a feather-duster.

I'm more the gal for acrobatics,
shedding knickers on the sofa.
I'd rather dance a wild fandango,
arms draped around a Spanish sailor,
than foxtrot with a vacuum-cleaner.

To hell with all this spit and polish,
the rub-a-dubbing, floors need scrubbing.
I'd rather find a well-bronzed beach boy,
slide through his legs and *oops-a-daisy* —
I wasn't born to hug a bucket.

Conundrum

That's us, our Golden Anniversary,
five years before your father died —
left me with this predicament:
we always ate our eggs well fried.

I thought today I'd poach my egg.
Your Dad would kick up such a fuss,
on second thoughts I'd better fry it,
anything else seems blasphemous.

What is it with you girls today?
All this loose sex and quick divorce?
We chose the captain, climbed on board,
felt duty-bound to stay the course.

In my day women knew their place,
your father had his fags and beer,
I had my kitchen and you kids,
the border-lines were all too clear:

I still make tea at four o'clock:
he'd watch the second hand and click
his fingers till I brought the tray,
God help me if the bread was thick!

At nine fifteen he'd click until
I brought his orange, peeled and pipped,
at ten he'd click again for milk:
I learned to keep my tongue well zipped.

We didn't talk of sex and stuff,
or kiss. He'd grunt and say come on
and I did. It kept him sweet:
I'm shot to pieces now he's gone.

The Tin Man

She's facing me, arms full of Japanese
sunflowers, legs apart, midriff bare,
a five-foot-nothing squall of home truths
that won't blow over. She's near to tears,

complains I've let her down. So what!
I've got the grand slam of a hangover,
oiled with a can or so of Master Brew.
Church bells clang my conscience –

sanctuary, a few bevvies in the pub
look great. She reads the signs. Whack!
A facelift of sunflowers pulls me up sharp.
And now there's pollen on her nose.

Somewhere in my head, a cell cracks open,
fertilized egg yolks flounder in a chipped mug,
she looks vulnerable, like a chick
squaring up to a cockerel. I'm stunned,

stopped in my tracks. Those jeans aren't meant
to keep secrets: she's pregnant, the thrill
of it shivers through me, quickens
my dulled conscience into life.

I want to hug her – her and the sunflowers,
build her a yellow brick dual-carriageway,
scattered with sunflower petals – but what if
sunflowers are a hard act to follow?

Disconnected

Dank Sunday,
River Kwai on the box again,
I give up, slope off
under dark skies, drift to the park
watch two glum ducks
quack round a drab pond.

Didn't think I'd see you here –
heard you'd left Dover for good,
found some new guy, gone to London.

... and now your warm glance,
your wind-flipped hair,
all but spark the damp fuse ...

I watch your mouth open on words,
close on a smile,
but all I hear are the honking ducks,
hungry for the crusts you toss.

This time there'll be no explosion:
we built our last bridge years ago.

The Second Eve

My first wife said (before divorce
had scarred our lives and left the lawyers
richer) that when I smiled, my lips
were like a twist of bitter-lemon.

You came towards me through the smell
of freshly-opened purple lilac —
a small woman, but tall inside,
with a smile to sweeten bitter aloe.

I was a hard-drinking man then,
a man who'd knocked the world about —
a man who'd taken what he wanted
and never felt the need to ask.

A man who needed nobody
or so the gin bottle proclaimed,
until the day you smiled at me
and my lips untwisted in reply.

Old Scores

The pampas grass is sparse and overgrown;
like ears of burnt-out wheat, it bends and breaks.
Damn and blast it, all I do is moan —
my windpipes wheeze and every muscle aches,
my head blanks when I bend to tie my shoe —
those bloody kids, I'll swing for them, I swear,
One each, I said and this is what they do,
they've stripped the trees, the Russet's bare.

I'll brain the buggers, give 'em such a clout,
they'll never scrump again and that's for sure,
but who the hell am I to cock a snout?
A man with bigger boots knocks at my door —
there'll be no bells, no candlesticks, no brass,
just open skies and waving pampas grass...

Higher Nature

Behind the Post Office, that's where she lives,
a handsome woman with a wooden leg,
russet hair as deep as leaves in autumn.
Her ruling passion's cosmic consciousness,
organic wholeness, bonding with the universe,
or so the doctor says and he should know:
his car is often seen outside the house.

But not a word about the wooden leg:
except to say he finds it most intriguing.
He's been acting rather strange these last few weeks,
stands for hours, embracing nature, arms outstretched,
rumour has it he sometimes does it naked.
The leg? Oh yes, the handsome woman claims
it's a miracle, a triumph of Higher Nature,
grafted on when she was still a child.
Her blood has mingled with the apple's sap:
she sheds her skin in winter to be reborn in spring.

I make her clothes: she wears those see-through things,
with suns and moons and planets where it counts –
and by the way, the limb is quite fantastic,
hand-carved from Da Vinci's 'Larynx and Leg'.
Don't quote me, but the doctor's wife is worried,
he's started burning incense, chanting *om..m..*
says that he seeks organic ecstasy.
And from the look of things I'd say he's found it.

Tree

I stand by the stump of the sycamore tree —
the one we called our wishing tree

and I climb up it as I did back then
to sit in the heart of the tree:

you follow me up and we mess around
as we always did in that cursed tree,

you wriggle about on a wind-warped limb:
I beg you be careful, you're shaking the tree,

but you laugh at me as you hang head down
monkey-like, from your branch in the tree —

a sudden crack, a piercing screech,
I lock my legs round a fork in the tree

as you slither to me and I grab your clothes
and we juggle together in the crook of the tree

and your shirt-tail rips and I lose my grip —
and there's no wishing left in the tree.

The Spirit of Christmas

The ragged Angel smiling down at me,
her radiant face unchanged from year to year,
harks back to Christmas 1953,

to presents piled beneath the well-lit tree,
to hot mince pies, washed down by ginger-beer.
The ragged Angel smiling down at me

ignites such frissons in my memory,
cuts through the tinsel strands to reappear,
harks back to Christmas 1953

when Mum bent down to pick up Timothy
and found him dead – our nursery crib his bier.
The ragged Angel smiling down at me

smiled at me then and just as vacantly;
that fixed demonic grin, that plastic sneer,
harks back to Christmas 1953.

The empty crib of our Nativity,
butchered our lives. For reasons yet unclear,
the ragged demon smiling down at me
harks back to Christmas 1953.

Pedestrian Crossing

There are mistakes you could choke on,
like the ones your parents tell new boyfriends:
painting uncle's greenhouse green –
windows, doors, compost bags,
tomatoes, peppers, orchids
and your new organza dress.

There are those you serve up
with the after-dinner mints,
like the one you made, when the Bishop
came to St Ursula's and innocently asked you
What would you like to be when you grow up?
and you said, *A belly-dancer.*

And those that send you scuttling
for the mouth-wash – like the time
you got mixed up with a chap at work,
swallowed every sugary word he said
till his wife turned up, with two kids
and a large slice of tongue pie ...

But what about that gin and tonic –
that last drink too many –
the one that furrowed your life,
narrowed your lips and shrivelled your brow?
A yellow coat, a squeal of brakes,
a muffled thump – the coat is red –
the lifelong cramps and stomach-aches
of living with a child that's dead.

Speak Again

People push in between my eyelids
past the flaming psychedelic lights:
sepia people, with dead-pan faces.
Crowds of them, like Trafalgar Square
on New Year's Eve, without the fun.

They don't shout or scream out loud,
elbow, jostle or fight
or ask who turned out the light.

They don't speak,
but the steady tread of their thin-soled shoes
and half-throttle heartbeats strumming the blues
unnerves me.

They crowd my space,
press themselves between my thoughts,
separate the strands, strip my emotions
to rags.

They don't speak, but I know them now,
from their art-work on my conscience:

I've visited their filthy cellars,
tasted food from dustbins,
slept in a cardboard box, stood on a bridge
daring myself to jump.

They don't speak because
there's no one to listen —
no one to ask...

Fragment

There's something creepy-odd about sunflowers,
that 'big brother' way they've got of watching you,
those seed-like unresponsive eyes, flat head
peering at you over garden walls, circling
sunwise as if to set their lens by it —
they got Van Gogh and now they're after you...

Dick Turpin *et al*

Bill Sykes, Jon Wild, Dick Turpin and all,
his head's so wide, he's extra tall.
He blackmails, bullies and knocks you off,
then hides behind his mother's shawl.

Turpin-et-al has taking ways,
when the stakes are high he always plays,
he borrows, begs, and sometimes lifts:
then blows his trumpet in self-praise,

He purloins, pilfers, pinches, nicks
my peppermints and paper clips,
then swears he only borrowed them
but now and then his memory slips.

That spiv, that swindler, webster, crook,
that man born with the devil's luck:
that brigand, bandit, and plagiarist
who dines out nightly on your book.

He plunders, rapes and pillages –
a lunatic when moonlight rages:
a swell, light-fingered, fiscal-thug,
a nightmare from the darker ages.

A pickpocket, a petty cutpurse,
it's hard to choose, when both mean worse.
Burglar, housebreaker, larcener:
his end's in sight, I've booked the hearse.

Learning to Spell

(or Longings of a Dyslexic Child 1945)

Miss Fanlyn said, *You're a lazy girl,*
you could learn to spell, if only you'd try.
Silly old faggot, no patience at all,
silly old faggot, what does she know?
When she talks to letters, they do as they're told,
but they're nasty and horrid and spiteful to me,
always dodging around and tripping me up.
Like the time when I wrote a poem about
the Which who couldn't decide witch way to go;
and Miss Fanlyn said, *It would have been good*
if you'd taken the trouble to find out witch which
was the which. So I told her I knew
a witch when I saw one and she sat
all my **Whiches** on bright red broomsticks
and my **Witch** ways on black-magic carpets
and she told the whole class, and I felt such a fool.
But I got my own back on her and the school
by showing them all exactly how well
a good-for-nothing-kid can spell:

I took the juice of a poppy,
the eye of a frog,
a clapped-out jalopy,
the coat of a dog,
a skeleton's smile,
a dromedary's hump,
an orang-utan's piles
and a warthog's lumps:
I boiled them up in frogspawn wine,
mumbled the words I couldn't spell
and multiplied them by ninety-nine,
turned the old faggot to a WITCH FROM HELL.

Dear Body

I've been conferring with L.B.
about the effects of the dialectics
of our emotions, those intense moments
of human happiness, when the world stands still
while we spin on our own axis —

L.B. reckons it's called freewheeling,
as opposed to the usual *crust*
handed out by life-chances, *crumbed*
by man's inhumanity to man —

I think it's closer to rocket fuel
because it can transport us to the stars
allow us to rewrite our personal horoscope,
choose between death in a human crater
and building our own space capsule.

We don't always see eye to eye,
but this time we're in accord;
our findings confirm that the brain
can incorporate the universe.

Ecstasy shouldn't be a pill.
Bearing that in mind, we've
upped your adrenalin supply,
the fourth dimension is the road past *Why*.

Your sincerely
R.B. (Right Brain)

Right Brained

Maybe it's because I'm right brained —
well that's what I think —
and I'm the one who has to read
the weirdo notes I leave myself:

...written it's before
poem the picture I if as
backward sentences writing like

And here I am, starting out from
where I've just arrived, unsure
whether I'm coming or going,
because, by the time I've re-routed
my sentences, I've missed the connection

arrived too late to write the poem
that imaged itself before
I blotted it out with words

Between Times

It started with a clock that emptied days,
whelming me somewhere in the outer-here
beside the ragged-edge of parting ways
where metaphors and images cohere
in ghoul-like gowns, then slowly disappear,
abscond with similes, lay blank and bare
the jig-saw pieces set beside the bier,
no coloured pictures; just a questionnaire

that I can't fill. What plane is this I'm on?
Light filters in, not much to see or hear,
a note or two of make-shift Mendelssohn;
no leitmotiv, no pitch to clue the ear,
just this innate belief that you are here.
Things slip and slide – silence and brash fanfare.
I'm stranded chord-less in a puzzle-sphere,
no clues as yet to pack this questionnaire.

I want to write, record the emptied hours,
explain death's unexpected change of gear;
write, *I love you* on the funeral flowers.
You can't see me, but seem to feel me near,
I flick your tie and brush away a tear
and whisper, *I am all and everywhere;
the what is, always was,* but you don't hear.
I have it now, love needs no questionnaire:

things are and aren't a true facsimile,
death's fifth dimension makes it extra clear:
time's concertina invites simile –
there's no duality, no shadows here.
Eternal doesn't rhyme with time – the near
and far are one: two halves are sure to pair.
The jig-saw pieces fit, colours cohere,
you need no chart, no maps, no questionnaire.

Thread

Cleopatra, Painted Lady —
Buddleia blooming *a priori* —
in camera the moment waits;
you rest a minute by my side,
then dip and dive and flutter by.
Your sequined T-Shirt calls to mind
the wing flip of a butterfly.

I catch you, kiss you, let you go —
my enigmatic Gemini —
your lips touch mine, a brief bouquet —
the time is right; the vortex swirls,
your amber eyes intensify,
I'm pinioned on the rim of chance —
the wing flip of a butterfly...

I Am a Woman Lying on a Leaf

(an arrangement of first lines from Philip Larkin)

Caught in the centre of a soundless field,
green-shadowed people sit, or walk in rings;
at once whatever happened starts receding –
I am a woman lying on a leaf.

Beyond all this the need to be alone,
climbing the hill within the deafening wind:
at once whatever happened starts receding,
sinking like sediment through the day.

Caught at the centre of a soundless field,
green-shadowed people sit, or walk in rings.
At once whatever happened starts receding,
the cloakroom pegs are empty now.

Beyond all this the need to be alone.
Tiny immortal streams are on the move:
at once whatever happened starts receding,
the trees are coming into leaf.

Caught in the centre of a soundless field,
my age fallen away, like white swaddling,
at once whatever happened starts receding:
I am a woman lying on a leaf.

Those Young English Lovers

(Musings on Sul Lago d' Orta – after Montale)

Where are they now who cried with the willow?
What can I make of this myriorama?
Did they build the bowers, envisage the tableau –

girl with a parasol, charming young fellow –
did they set the stage for their melodrama,
where are they now who cried with the willow?

What did they do to deserve this tomorrow,
the damp and decay of this sad panorama?
Did they build the bowers, envisage the tableau?

Did they sit beneath the marble gazebo,
were there tearful tirades, was there personal drama?
Where are they now who cried with the willow?

Was she an heiress? Was he a gigolo?
Did he deceive her, intending to harm her?
Did they build the bowers, envisage the tableau?

Is this her face in expressionless cameo,
framed in a locket of Kismet or Karma?
Where are they now who cried with the willow?
Did they build the bowers, envisage the tableau?

*Written in response to a challenge to winning poets of the Poetry on the Lake
Competition (2005) who were sent the Italian poem, Sul Largo d'Orta by Eugenio Montale.*

Nothing Original

                          This poem
borrows autumn from Keats,
no one can beat his first stanza:
it's misty and the fruit's ripe.

If it haunts you, and it will,
it's because it mentions Emma,
who's gone, but still calls me:

my Em's dress was cerulean,
her hair the colour of ripe corn
we shared one heady Hardy summer,
moments when waves of colour mixed
with sparrow calls and, in my case,
a bull that jumped the five-bar gate.

Hardy's woman had a blue dress –
blue that's sort of heavenly:

the brain is wider than the sky.

Boy, that woman knew a thing or two,
that's Emily, Emily Dickinson, not my Em –
typical woman though – always talking
about something you can't lay your fingers
on – there I go, bull-rushing again:
the brain is wider than the sky –

it was Madonna blue that night. I tasted
the smell of apples on her breath,
the mushroom freshness of her skin – she
'rowed me to Eden' with one stroke of my oar...

Chocolate Thoughts

Deceitful as a chocolate layer-cake,
four times as seductive, six times sweeter,
full of additives and excess hormone levels,
the sort of woman who makes you feel guilty
because you don't go for extra-marital sex,
wear wonderbras and cheekless see-through thongs.

Impulsive. Full of wannabes and going-to's
and soft-centred butter-wouldn't-melt why-
shouldn't-I's that leave you feeling guilty
as if you've tasted something you shouldn't have
and it's left you torpid, sluggish, over-full,
but moreish, always moreish. Wanting to be like her.
Wondering why you always linger on the edge –
drooling for a slice of life.

By the same author
The Sorcerer's Arc (Hearing Eye, 2004)

For information about forthcoming publications, or our new catalogue of books (1987–2007), please send an SSAE. All orders are attended to by return of post. You may also like to see our website where you can order all our books online.

Hearing Eye, Box 1, 99 Torriano Avenue, London, NW5 2RX
Tel: 0207 267 2751 or email: books@hearingeye.org

www.hearingeye.org